Beside Still Waters

Discovering Peace In The Midst of Your Child's Addiction:

A Guide for Mothers of Addicts

by:
Cherri Freeman
Love Them To Life

Beside Still Waters

ISBN: 978-0-9962471-0-8

Cover Concept by Ali Pavuk
Photo by Cherri Freeman
Cover by Mark Phillips
mark@marksphillips.com

Formatted by:
Cathy Solomon
cathgfi@gmail.com

Printed by:
Lightning Source, Inc.
1246 Heil Quaker Blvd.
La Vergne, TN 37086 USA

Published by XL Project
31A Yorktowne Pkwy
Whiting, NJ 08759
lovethemtolife@gmail.com

Unless otherwise noted, all Scripture references were taken from the English Standard Version (Crossway Publishers).

DEDICATION

This book was born out of the pain of being the mother of children who had lost their way and stumbled into the seeming abyss of addiction. Although that pain is fierce, I am grateful to God for using my experiences to help other mothers as they walk through deep waters.

I would like to dedicate this book to my husband, Joe, for encouraging me to write and for freely sharing his expertise gained through his many years of addiction, his personal transformation, and now through his counseling practice.

Joe, thank you for patiently standing by me as I have worked through these issues and for looking over my writing with a gently critical eye to make sure the truths were expressed as clearly, firmly, and as lovingly as possible. Thank you for being a man of God, for your passion for truth and integrity, for persevering through pain, and for loving me unconditionally. I am blessed to have you as my husband.

Many thanks to Cathy Solomon for her hours of work formatting this book. We couldn't have done it without you, Cathy.

Thanks also to Dr. John Woodward for his editing, mentoring, and constant support.

Beside Still Waters

TABLE OF CONTENTS

Beside Still Waters

INTRODUCTION

The Lord is my Shepherd, I shall not want. He makes me lie down in green pastures. He leads me beside the still waters. He restores my soul. Yes, though I walk through the valley of the shadow of death, I will fear no evil, for you are with me (Psalm 23:1-4).

As a mom who deeply loves her children, including those who have been caught in the idolatry of addiction, I often feel as if there are no still waters in my life. The cascading torrents of trouble pour on relentlessly with no end in sight, or at least it seems that way. Where are those still waters? Mothers of addicts walk through the valley of the shadow of death every day. There is the death of hopes and dreams, the death of trust and integrity, and the potential of overdose every time they get high. There is palpable fear along with the desire to control the situation, to make everything somehow work out okay.

My prayer for you is that you will find those still waters in the arms of the God who loves you more than you could possibly know. While these are not exhaustive studies on each topic, may they help you learn to work through the tough issues surrounding addiction in a healthy way. Life doesn't always work out the way we dreamed it would, but you can rest in His faithfulness, His sovereignty, and trust in His never-ending love for your child and for you.

Nevertheless, I am continually with You; You hold my right hand. You guide me with your counsel, and afterward You will receive me to glory. Whom have I in heaven but You? And there is nothing on earth that I desire besides You. My flesh and my heart may fail, but God is the strength of my heart and my portion forever (Psalm 73:23-26 ESV)

Please note that a facilitator's guide is available as a download on the *Love Them to Life* website:

www.lovethemtolife.com

Chapter 1

THE ANATOMY OF ADDICTION

"Why can't my child just stop doing drugs or drinking? He knows it is harmful and he says he wants to stop but he keeps making bad choices."

All of us have our own 'addictions,' to some extent (especially when it comes to chocolate!), but unless we personally have been in chemical addiction, it is difficult to understand the slavery it brings.

Gerald May, M.D., in his book, *Addiction and Grace*, defines addiction as follows:

Addiction is a state of compulsion, obsession, or preoccupation that enslaves a person's will and desire.

There are many different types of addiction, but they primarily fall into three categories:

1. addiction to a chemical substance(s), such as alcohol, drugs, tobacco, food, or caffeine.
2. addiction to a behavior, such as shopping, sex, pornography, gambling, work, sports, and others.
3. addiction to relationships, such as codependency or domination/abuse of another person.

It is crucial for moms to understand addiction in order to better know how to deal with their children, no matter what age they are. Many moms are dealing with adult offspring who are in their 40s, 50s, and even 60s and are still asking to live at home or asking for money.

Gerald May states that there are five essential characteristics of addiction:

- tolerance
- withdrawal symptoms
- self-deception
- loss of willpower
- distortion of attention

1. Tolerance: when people use a certain substance long enough, they become used to it. More of that substance is needed to get the same effects.

2. Withdrawal symptoms: when a person stops an addictive substance, the body goes through withdrawal, causing nervous system reactions such as irritability, agitation, increased pulse rate, tremors, and panic. There is also a rebound effect that causes opposite types of symptoms from the prior effect of the drug. Rebound from a depressant drug will cause hyperactivity and so on.

3. Self-deception: the person is often deluded into thinking they are safe and can stop at any time. They use the techniques of rationalization, minimization, and denial to persuade themselves that they are okay.

4. Loss of willpower: one part of addiction that makes it so difficult for loved ones to understand is that the person's will is essentially divided in two. One part of the will is sick of living that life and wants to get better. The other part of the will, which is most often stronger, wants to still continue in the addiction. The person may make repeated resolutions to stop the destructive behavior. Every time the resolutions fail, the addiction becomes more powerful. The Apostle Paul, in Romans 7:15-24,

describes so well the conflict of will when he talks about doing the things he does not want to do and not doing the things he knows he should. He finally cries out in agony:

> *Oh wretched man that I am! Who will deliver me from this body of death?*

According to Dr. May, if a person can simply will themselves to stop, they are not truly addicted.

5. Distortion of attention: finding the next fix or the next drink becomes all-consuming, to the exclusion of all other needs and responsibilities, including health, finances, food, family, relationships, and certainly God.

The essence of addiction is the sin of idolatry: worshiping the next fix and sacrificing everything in order to get it. Every time we try to fill the hole in our souls with anything other than God, it is a form of addiction and is a destructive stronghold.

QUESTIONS:

1. When did you first suspect that your child was addicted? How did you feel?

2. What does the phrase 'addiction as idolatry' mean to you? Can you see areas of your own life that could become addictions?

3. Codependency is an addiction as much as drug or alcohol use. Is it possible that 'helping' your child could be an addiction in your life?

PRAYER:

Father, we need to be wise in understanding our children's addictions and clearly seeing the battle that is going on for their very lives. Please give us wisdom as we seek to assist them to brokenness so that they will surrender to You.

Chapter 2

THE PATHWAY OF CHEMICAL ADDICTION

Chemical addiction, which is addiction to drugs and/or alcohol, often follows a series of stages. It is helpful to understand and demystify these stages as we deal with our kids.

Jeff Van Vonderen, in his book *Hope and Help for the Addicted*, talks about addiction starting with experimentation. Often it begins with our kids' peers who have tried a drug or drink, described the experience, and have awakened a curiosity in our children as to whether it will cause the same effect in them. They want to know what it feels like to be drunk or high. It can also start with the peer pressure of not being 'cool' if they don't try things. Often the desire to experiment is accompanied by low self-esteem, family stress, school stress, loss of a dating relationship, or other emotional trauma. The desire is to be able to control how they feel by what they use.

The next stage is functional use. They continue using recreationally without suffering consequences of job loss, broken relationships, or legal issues.

The 'slippery slope' of addiction gets steeper when the person uses the drugs or alcohol to numb the heavy emotions of guilt, shame, and remorse they may experience as the consequences begin to catch up with them in every area of their life (stage three). They experience an inability to stop their descent.

The last stage is full-fledged addiction, which is characterized by a complete loss of control. They chase the 'high' but find it less and less often, as tolerance to the chemical increases. Using becomes more about avoiding withdrawal sickness rather than getting high. They experience the loss of finances and relationships as well as legal issues and begin dealing drugs in order to support their habit. They have become slaves to drugs or alcohol, but more importantly, they have become slaves to self, sin, and strongholds.

Proverbs 23:29-35 describes so well the experience of a drunk or high person:

Who has woe?
Who has sorrow?
Who has contentions?
Who has complaints?
Who has wounds without cause?
Who has redness of eyes?
Those who linger long at the wine. Those who go in search of mixed wine.
Do not look on the wine when it is red, when it sparkles in the cup, when it swirls around smoothly;
At the last it bites like a serpent, and stings like a viper.
Your eyes will see strange things, and your heart will utter perverse things.
Yes, you will be like the one who lies down in the midst of the sea, or like one who lies at the top of the mast, saying: "They have struck me, but I was not hurt; they have beaten me, but I did not feel it. When shall I awake, that I may seek another drink?"

What can we do to help our kids as we see them self-destructing? Prayer, prayer, and more prayer would be the first thing. Then assist them to brokenness, which means allowing them to feel the consequences of their decisions. It is so painful to watch the process. Finding your identity and strength in your relationship with Jesus Christ is not only *an* answer, it is *the* only answer.

QUESTIONS:

1. Read Psalm 73: 23-26. Why is it important to experience God as the strength of your heart?

2. What stage do you think your child is currently at in his/her addiction? How have you handled the emotions of seeing him/her self-destruct?

3. What do you think it means to 'assist them to brokenness'? What are some practical ways of assisting them to brokenness?

PRAYER:

Father, You are the only true answer for my child's addiction. Please give me the wisdom I need as I love my child through this difficult time.

Chapter 3

KING BABY

Have you ever wondered why your children make such irresponsible choices, completely the opposite of how you raised them?

There is a idea that says that people stop maturing at the age they started into their addiction. The person may be in an adult's body but continue to act as a 15-year-old child. This is called the King Baby Syndrome, which will help shed some light on why our children act as they do.

Although this is not a complete discussion of King Baby, the following are the core characteristics:

- They are irresponsible yet attracted to responsible people who compensate for them.
- They are easily angered, especially at authority.
- They are the 'Class clown'—they enjoy making others laugh as a distraction from their destructive, irresponsible behavior.
- They don't handle money and financial decisions well.
- They manipulate you into doing what they want you to do.
- They want your time when they need you but you don't hear from them when they are okay.
- Frustration and anger immobilize them. They don't handle adversity well.
- They blame others for their situation.
- They have big plans but little to no follow-through.

- They have a strong fear of abandonment and rejection.
- They intimidate people to make themselves feel important.
- They want immediate gratification.

The three main idols of a King Baby (whether male or female) are pleasure, power, and attention. Ultimately, it is all about serving self: I want what I want when I want it.

King Baby is, in many ways, a very dark version of the movie *Big*, in which a young boy ends up in a man's body. His behavior was appropriate for his emotional age but completely inappropriate for his body's age. In the same way, our children who are in addiction look as if they should be able to think and act in mature ways, while, in reality, they have stopped growing emotionally and do not make good decisions.

Does this idea of King Baby make the addict less responsible for their actions? Not at all. They need to be held responsible for their choices in order for them to reach the point of brokenness. Once they are clean and sober, the process of growth and maturation can take place, especially as they learn their true identity in Christ.

1 Peter 2:2 says,

Like newborn babies, crave pure spiritual milk, so that by it you may grow up in your salvation.

There is hope for our kids. They can become men and women of God, no matter what they have done or how long they have been addicted.

QUESTIONS:

1. What characteristics of King Baby do you see in your son or daughter?

2. What are some of the frustrations you have experienced with your child as it relates to King Baby?

3. What are some techniques that you could use to hold your child responsible for their actions?

PRAYER:

Father, we crave for our children to find freedom and maturity through You. We trust You to work in them as we continue to love them and pray for them.

Chapter 4

CODEPENDENCY

One of the most difficult topics to write about for me personally is the topic of codependency. As I look back over the years of my son's addiction, I can see so many things I would have done differently. It is so easy for a mom to be codependent and not realize it at all.

It is important to understand what codependency is so that we can identify it and stop it before it destroys our lives and those around us. Wikipedia says,

> A 'codependent' is loosely defined as someone who exhibits too much, and often inappropriate, caring for persons who depend on him or her. A 'codependent' is one side of a relationship between mutually needy people. The dependent, or obviously needy party(ies), may have emotional, physical, or financial difficulties, or addictions they seemingly are unable to surmount. The 'codependent' party exhibits behavior that controls, makes excuses for, pities, and takes other actions to perpetuate the obviously needy party's condition because of their desire to be needed and fear of doing anything that would change the relationship.

A codependent person will try to control the person who is addicted in order to change their behavior. Unfortunately, no amount of emotion or threats will cause anyone caught in addiction to quit. Control can not change a person's heart, even if restrictions are placed on their behavior.

Jeff Van Vonderen, in his book *Hope and Help for the Addicted*, defines a codependent as

a person who seeks to get his/her sense of well-being from the dependent loved one.

He also says that codependency is

feeding the behavior of an individual who is causing pain or stress to the whole unit or group.

According to Van Vonderen, there are three factors which contribute to being codependent:

1. You have to care deeply about the person.
2. You don't understand addiction and chemical dependency.
3. You feel a sense of shame about yourself, as if you are not a person of value or are in some way deficient. You don't see your performance as being as good as others, so your value goes down and your shame increases (in your eyes). You try to compensate for that shame by 'helping'.

Van Vonderen says:

Codependency is an addiction that results from an idolatrous relationship with someone who is chemically dependent. A codependent person turns to something other than God as his/her source of well-being. If another human being is your false god, you do not want a broken god who is drunk, irresponsible, and causes embarrassment. You want a sober and responsible god, one that will cause you to feel proud. Therefore, you must fix your god, which is why so much time and energy, his/

her own and other people's, is spent by the codependent trying to fix the chemically dependent person.

It is so easy for a mom to slip unknowingly into the addiction of codependency because we naturally take care of our kids, even after they get older. However, it is easy to allow our kids to become idols in our lives and most likely are completely unaware of it. We try to compensate for their problems and pick them up when they fall. When I paid my son's fines and bailed him out of numerous situations, I thought I was helping him get on 'level ground' so that he could start making good choices. It didn't happen that way, and I kept him from feeling the consequences of his choices. I thought I was doing the loving things but did not understand that my actions were motivated by guilt for choices I had made that had affected him. It was also motivated by people-pleasing tendencies. Wikihow.com says,

Are we enabling unacceptable behavior in order for us to appease that person (who is causing disruption) in order for us not to be rejected, confronted, challenged, or hated by them?

Identifying the problem is the first step to getting well. From where do you get your value? Is it wrapped up in your kids' achievements, your job, your husband, your ministry, your performance in any area of life? If so, you are on a slippery slope to pain, depression, and codependency. You have value because God sees you as valuable. Colossians 3:4 says,

And when Christ, who is your real life, is revealed to the whole world, you will share in all His glory.

My identity is based on who He is, not who I am, and especially not what my child does, which is the most freeing thing in the world. When I 'accept my acceptance,' that Jesus will never love me any more or any less no matter what my performance is, I can be healthy enough to truly love my child in a way that does not enable his/her addiction. Love them to life!

QUESTIONS:

1. What is the difference between nurturing and codependency?

2. Jeff Van Vonderen lists three ingredients to being codependent. What are they and how are they relevant to your situation?

3. How would you define shame? Why would shame contribute to codependency?

4. a. What is meant by 'people-pleasing'? How does people-pleasing relate to codependency?

    b. Read Galatians 1:10 to see what God says about people-pleasing.

5. List some ways you can begin the process of healthy relationships instead of codependency.

PRAYER:

Lord, I want my identity to be in You and not in pleasing those around me at all cost. Please help me to recognize that my life is in You only, no matter what happens with my child. I need Your help to love _____ to life.

Chapter 5

ENABLING

The dictionary defines enabling as:

to make able, to supply with the means, knowledge, or opportunity; to make possible.

People who enable dysfunctional behavior are said to be codependent, in that there is a sense of self-esteem and well being that can come from 'helping' someone else.

How does this relate to moms whose children are in addiction? We carried them inside of us for nine months. We went through the pain of labor and delivery and spent our time making sure that they were safe, fed, and cared for. We rocked them to sleep, sang them lullabies, read them books, and kissed away their cuts and scrapes. We read them Bible stories and prayed with them. We did everything we could to make their life better.

And then the call comes from the police station that they have been arrested for drugs or alcohol. We think it is just a teenage phase, pay their fines because they don't have any money, cajole/encourage them to change their friends, go to church more, do the 'right' things. None of it works and they sink deeper into the mess they have made. More arrests, more fines, more promises to change—all in vain. We pay for attorneys, send them to treatment centers, allow them to live at home, give them money when they 'need' it; all the while, they plunge deeper into hard-core addiction.

We look at our nieces and nephews, as well as our friends' kids, who are going to college, getting graduate degrees, getting married, and having kids. We look at our own child who just keeps getting thinner and thinner, with pasty skin color and straggly hair, and wonder where we went wrong.

How do we know if we are enabling or just providing the kind of love that encourages good choices? How do we get past the pain of choices we made that may have led to the feelings our children are trying to drown with drugs or alcohol? Do we 'owe' them help to get out of trouble?

When we make the courageous choice to love our kids to life, not to death, there are some 'tough love' decisions that need to be made. Loving them doesn't necessarily feel good and will inevitably incur their wrath as they realize that mom is not going to do things for them anymore. One of the most painful experiences of my life was changing the locks on my door, knowing that my jewelry had been stolen and pawned for drug money. Another was getting a call that my son had left a drug rehab early and was told he had to walk, despite it being late winter and several hundred miles from home. The picture of him sleeping in the woods with no blankets, no food, and in freezing temperatures was intolerable. And yet, not allowing him to feel the consequences of his choices in the past had allowed him to continue his downward spiral. I had to tell him I could not help him. It was a terrible time for me, as I knew he could freeze to death. I also knew that I could get the dreaded call that he had overdosed and died if I did not allow him to experience the consequences of his choices.

PsychologyToday.com has a list of enabling behaviors:

1.   Do you often ignore unacceptable behavior?

2.   Do you find yourself resenting the responsibilities you have taken on?

3. Do you consistently put your own needs and desires aside in order to help someone else?

4. Do you have trouble expressing your own emotions?

5. Do you ever feel fearful that not doing something will cause a blowup, make the person leave you, or even result in violence?

6. Do you ever lie to cover for someone else's mistakes?

7. Do you consistently assign blame for problems to other people rather than the one who is really responsible?

8. Do you continue to offer help when it is never appreciated or acknowledged?

The first task is to take a close, honest look at your patterns and the emotions that go along with them. Facing our need to be liked and loved is a huge step in getting well. It is very important to have someone who can talk honestly with you about what they see and/or have a support group to hold you accountable. The most important thing is to know how deeply loved you are by God and that He is with you every step of the way. He wants us to entrust our children to Him, to take our hands off the situation, and to let Him work in their life without our interference. You have value because God sees you as valuable.

QUESTIONS:

1. What is the relationship between enabling and codependency?

2. Could providing a place to live for a child who is actively addicted be considered enabling? What are some other things you do or have done that could be considered enabling?

3. What are some steps you can take now to stop enabling?

4. Where do we find the courage and peace to stop enabling? Read Isaiah 43:1-2 and put your own name in.

PRAYER:

Father, please help me to understand that love and enabling are not the same. Please help me to truly love by not accepting unacceptable behavior, by standing for truth and honesty, and by refusing to love my child to death. Please give me the courage to say 'no' when I need to and the peace to know that I can't control my child's choices.

Chapter 6

DENIAL

It is easy, as the old saying goes, to 'bury your head in the sand' and not want to see the signs of addiction that are staring you in the face. Denial is defined as when

a person is faced with a fact that is too uncomfortable to accept and rejects it instead, insisting that it is not true despite what may be overwhelming evidence (Oxford English Dictionary).

Denial could be simple denial, in which the person won't accept the fact at all, or it could involve minimizing the seriousness of the situation.

Why do we deny? Some possible reasons are:

- Embarrassment/pride
- Fear of condemnation by friends and family
- Fear of conflict with our children
- We don't know what to do so it is easier to do nothing

Denying your children's addiction puts you in the 'nation of -ations': minimization, rationalization, and justification, to name a few. It contributes to the problem of enabling. Until we face the facts and take the tough steps needed to confront the problem, we are potentially contributing to their death. Confrontation doesn't make us popular; if your identity is wrapped up in your child's approval, pleasing them rather than God, it will be tempting to deny the seriousness of the situation. How much better for our child's sake would it be for us to see things for how they are and not what we want them to be (see Galatians 1:10).

Ephesians 4: 14-15 says,

Then we will no longer be infants, tossed back and forth by the waves, and blown here and there by every wind of teaching and by the cunning and craftiness of people in their deceitful scheming. Instead, speaking the truth in love, we will grow to become in every respect the mature body of Him who is the head, that is, Christ.

The most loving thing we can do is to face the truth and speak it in love. The choice they make is then entirely their own.

QUESTIONS:

1. Discuss what is meant by the "nation of -ations;" minimization, rationalization, and justification. Have there been situations in which you, or someone you know, have minimized, rationalized, or justified someone's behavior?

2.   How does denial contribute to enabling?

3.   How do you handle uncomfortable situations, such as when you are faced with evidence of addiction?

4.   You have discovered drug paraphernalia in your child's room. What does 'speaking the truth in love' look like in this situation?

PRAYER:

Father, I want to know the truth, as You have promised that the truth will set me free. Please help me to speak the truth in love to my child.

Chapter 7

PATTERNS OF ADDICTIVE BEHAVIOR

It is very important for us to recognize signs that our kids are chemically dependent (addicted). The following is a list of common patterns for people in addiction:

- Changes in sleep patterns, such as sleeping all day, awake all or most of the night
- Money missing from the house
- Jewelry missing
- Medications missing
- Apathy, not caring about work or schoolwork, activities, old friends, athletics
- Always needing money, asking to borrow or have money given
- Argumentative
- New friends, street-wise friends
- Nodding out
- Problems at school, grades slipping, dropping out of activities
- Appearance changes, not caring about hygiene or clothing
- Physical health issues
- Behavioral and relationship changes
- Depression
- 'Street' talk
- Loss of appetite, weight loss
- Unable to look you in the eye

If you suspect chemical dependency, it is important to speak up and ask questions. If you close your eyes and hope things will get better, they will undoubtedly get worse. Many parents hesitate to search their child's room for evidence of drug use. It is imperative that you do this. The right to privacy ends when a child is in danger and is endangering the whole household.

Keep your eyes open for the following items:

- Cigar wrappers
- Aluminum foil, especially if it has black smudges on it
- Black smudges on door handles, furniture, clothing, etc.
- Brillo pads, Chore Boy copper pads
- Cotton balls and Q tips (used as filters when shooting up)
- Spoons, especially with burnt residue and cotton balls
- Bottle caps
- Plastic bottles with holes burnt in them
- Empty pen casings or straws
- Pills and bags of powder
- Small baggies with stamped names on them
- Bags of vegetation (pot)
- Pipes and glass stems
- Syringes

QUESTIONS:

1. How do you feel about searching your child's room if you suspect drug or alcohol use?

2. If you find any drug paraphernalia or suspicious objects, what should you do?

3. How would you handle a confrontation with your child in a healthy, godly way? (Suggestion: divide into groups and role-play a confrontation)

4.   Read Ephesians 4:15. How do we practice 'speaking the truth in love'?

5.   If you confront your child with solid evidence of chemical dependency and he/she refuses to get help, what should your next steps be? Especially when the chemically dependent person is not a minor, have you faced the possibility of telling him/her to find another place to live?

PRAYER:

Father, in our wildest dreams we never expected to have to face this issue and feel so inadequate to deal with it. Thank you that You are adequate for every situation, even when we feel as if our hearts are being ripped out. We need your peace, comfort, and courage to do what is best for our child who is in bondage, even if it is tough.

Chapter 8

STEALING

You may think that your son or daughter would never steal from you, but with addiction comes the desperation to finance the habit. The fear of going into withdrawal sickness is even more powerful than the urge to get high. Money, jewelry, electronics, medications, and anything else that can be pawned is not safe in your home if your child is addicted. Please don't make the mistake of thinking it will never happen to you. It is not a matter of *if* it will happen but a matter of *when*.

There is a sense of shock, betrayal, and grief that goes along with finding out your child has stolen from you. Sometimes you are able to find items at the pawn shop if the theft is discovered quickly enough. However, very often heirloom jewelry is gone forever by the time you realize what has happened. One mother recently found out that her son had stolen his grandfather's wedding ring that he had worn for 54 years. By the time the theft was discovered, the ring was gone forever. There is a sense of loss more from the sentimental value than the actual monetary value, as well as a feeling of betrayal that your child would take something so meaningful and irreplaceable from you.

It is important that we hold 'things' loosely, in the sense that they do not become idols in our life. It is also important that we allow ourselves to grieve the loss of innocence and trust when we realize the depths to which our child has sunk.

Suggestions:

1. Get a safe and keep the key on you at all times. Lock up your medications.
2. Change the locks on your house.
3. Don't leave your wallet, credit cards, or financial information accessible.
4. Prosecute them if they steal from you. As difficult as this would be, it may wake your child up and save them from going further into addiction. Tough love is still love.
5. Have a list of your electronics and other valuables, including bicycles. Pictures and product numbers are helpful in identifying recovered items or for putting in claims to insurance.

QUESTIONS:

1. Have you discovered any theft in your home? How did it make you feel?

2. At what level of stealing would you consider reporting your child to the police?

3. If your child has stolen from you, how did you deal with the situation? What advice would you give to someone who is just starting to go through life with an addicted child?

4. Where do you go when you experience loss, betrayal, and grief? Read Isaiah 53:4a.

PRAYER:

Father, I cannot comprehend that my child whom I love so much would steal from me and yet I know that it can happen. Please give me the wisdom and the courage to confront the situation the way You would want me to.

Chapter 9

LEGAL ISSUES

You are awakened in the middle of the night by a phone call from the police station. Your child has been arrested for possession of a controlled and dangerous substance (CDS) or for DUI and your stomach drops. You are in shock. You may never have had any experience with the legal system and, therefore, have no idea what to do in this situation. This is not meant to be legal advice; however, if you are the mom of someone involved with drugs, it is not a matter of *if* he will have legal problems, it is a matter of *when*.

Most likely your first question is whether they are safe in jail. Your children are actually safer than when they are out on the streets. And being arrested can be the wake-up call that is needed for both you and your child that there is a major problem.

Some of the emotions you may feel are anger, fear, humiliation, confusion, and shock. You want to get him out of jail as quickly as possible, but it is important to think through the issues.

1. They may be released "ROR" (released on their own recognizance). This means that there is no bail required to have them released until they go before the judge.

2. There may be bail set by the judge. The court may require 10% down or the full amount of the bail in order to release them. People often use a bail bondsman to post bail and

47

may be required to use their house as collateral if they choose to do so. If your child chooses to leave town and not show up at court, you could lose your house. It is very important that you not devastate yourself financially to get him out of the mess he created so that he feels the effects of the choices he has made. One way to help him feel those effects is to not bail him out, even if it is his first offense. He needs time to realize that the path he is on is not a good path. It may make the difference between loving your child to life and not to death.

3. If your child was arrested for DUI or drug possession and she was driving your car, it could potentially be impounded, especially if she has enough quantity of drugs on her person and/or in the car to qualify her as a dealer (possession with intent to distribute). *NEVER LOAN YOUR CAR TO YOUR CHILDREN if you know they are using or drinking!*

4. The question will come up regarding getting a public defender vs. a private attorney. Again, it is important that you not devastate your finances to hire a lawyer in order to 'prove your love' for your child. This is a decision you will have to make depending on your circumstances, but you are not being unloving if you don't hire a private attorney and instead use a public defender.

These are very tough issues. I never thought I would face them but have done so repeatedly. It is heartbreaking and humiliating. Find someone who has been through this and can help you think objectively. Pray for wisdom (James 1:5). Most importantly, make sure that your identity and security are in Jesus, the One who will never leave you nor forsake you. Trust Him with your child, no matter what happens.

QUESTIONS:

1. Has your child had legal issues? If so, how did that make you feel? Did you think you had to get your child out of jail right away at all cost?

2. What do you think about the idea of bail the first time being mercy and the second time being enabling? Is mercy in the case of a first offense the best choice, in your opinion, or is it more loving to assist them to brokenness by leaving them in jail?

3. How has your child's legal issues affected your health, finances, and relationships?

4. If you are married, how do you and your husband decide about handling legal issues? Has this area caused problems in your relationship?

PRAYER:

Father, we never, ever thought we would see our children in jail and yet their choices have taken them there. I ask for protection for our children. Would you also make our children uncomfortable enough that they will get the 'wake-up call' they need? Please help them know how much we love them.

Chapter 10

RELATIONSHIPS

It has been said that most addicts think that they are only hurting themselves with their choices, while in reality they are hurting at least four or five people, usually family members. Having an addicted person in the family, especially if they are living in the home, changes the family dynamics. It can feel as if the life has been sucked out of the family unit. There can be major financial stress, as well as interpersonal stress.

You, as the mom of an addict, may feel as if you are caught in the middle. If you are married to the father of your child, you hopefully have a partner and a support person to go with you through the decisions and struggles. However, there may not be agreement as to the best way to handle things and this can cause a rift in the marriage relationship. One of you may tend to be more enabling and the other more toward the tough love side. It is important that you get help from a pastor or counselor as the two of you walk through this difficult time so that you can build your marriage and not tear it down. It is crucial that you display a united front to your child, even if behind the scenes you don't always agree. There are deep emotions that may be expressed in harmful ways as you walk through the turbulent waters of a child self-destructing. Addicts are master manipulators and seem to be able to lie without feeling remorse. Trusting each other, respecting and valuing your differences, keeping each other in first place after God, and making the commitment to protect your marriage are so important to surviving this difficult time.

A different dynamic occurs if you are remarried and dealing with blended family issues. It is much easier for a stepfather to take a hard line with a stepchild. You may feel that you have to be in the middle to protect your child, or you may agree with the decision on how to handle the situation but not agree with the way it is presented to your child (perhaps in anger/rage). These issues have the potential to split a marriage if they are not talked through, especially if you feel more allegiance to your child than to your husband or you feel he is too harsh or is unjust. Again, being able to love, value, and respect your mate, as well as feeling valued, respected, and loved yourself are the pillars of a strong relationship. Above all, putting and keeping Christ in the center of the relationship is the cement that holds it together. I would recommend reading *Families Where Grace Is In Place* by Jeff VanVonderen and *The Meaning of Marriage* by Timothy and Kathy Keller.

You may be a single mom who has to deal with an enabling former spouse or who has no one with whom to share the burden of the situation. Finding your security, wisdom, and peace from the One who loves you the most, your Abba God, is the only answer to the pain you are experiencing. It is important to have a support group of friends and family around you.

Siblings are profoundly affected by a brother or sister in addiction. They may not get the attention that they need, as all the attention is focused on the addict. They may try to compensate for the way their addicted sibling is acting by trying to be perfect and not cause any grief. They may withdraw from family interaction. It is very important that each member of the family gets the help and attention that they need, not just the member who is 'acting out'.

Colossians 3: 3-4 says,

For you have died and your life is hidden with Christ in God. When Christ, who is our life, is revealed, then you also will be revealed with Him in glory.

When Christ is our very life, nothing can shake us to the core of our being. When our relationships are founded in Him, He is the rock of the family that will not be moved. Things may still be difficult and hurtful, but nothing can shake the foundation if we are focused on Him.

QUESTIONS:

1. Describe your family situation. Is it blended? Are you a single mom?

2. What are ways you have seen relationships suffer in your family due to addiction?

3. What are some ways to support your other children when a sibling is in addiction?

4. What are ways you can protect your marriage from the stresses of dealing with an addicted child?

PRAYER:

Father, we need to keep the balance in our relationships. We need You to be first, our spouse second, and our kids third. Life becomes completely unmanageable when we lose that balance. We need Your help and Your wisdom to keep the love relationship in our marriage going strong despite the stress we feel. Thank you for caring about every area of our life.

Chapter 11

WORRY

Worry is like a cancer that kills our peace and joy. We can spend our lives worrying about our kids, finances, health, relationships, jobs, and on and on. Have you ever watched a hamster run on the wheel in the cage? Worrying becomes that wheel. You get on and run and run but you never get anywhere. I have a habit of waking up early and lying in bed for a few minutes before getting up, praying and thinking through the day ahead. So often the enemy fills my mind with things to worry about. Instead of feeling refreshed from the night's sleep, I am troubled, uncomfortable, and stressed by the morning's 'wheel' of worry.

Jesus talks in John 15 about abiding in Him. If we accept the truth of His love and His power, why do we think that worrying will change the outcome of the day? (Matt 6:27) It all comes down to trust. I either trust Him with EVERYTHING, that He is intimately aware and involved in every aspect of my life, or I don't trust Him and think that I have to take care of everything, which ends up being a disaster. We especially need to trust Him when things don't go the way we want them to go, including when we see our kids making poor choices and heading down a road of destruction. We need to trust Him when our decision to stop enabling leads to tough situations and anger on the part of our kids. When we understand that He knows the whole picture and is constantly working for our good (Romans 8:28), we can relax and get off the wheel of worry.

Trust is the antidote to the poison of worry.

QUESTIONS:

1. What things do you worry about?

2. How difficult is it to function when you are consumed with worry? How does it affect your other relationships when you are worried about your child?

3. What are some practical ways that you have found to deal with worry?

PRAYER:

Father, when I can't get off the wheel of worry, I need You to settle my mind. I need to trust You with absolutely everything in my life. I know that You love my child even more than I do. I give _____ to You and trust You, no matter what happens.

Chapter 12

GUILT AND REMORSE

Is it my fault that my child is an addict? Should I have disciplined him more or less? Did my personal choices cause such pain in him that he turned to this?

These are the inevitable questions that go through a mom's mind over and over. How could the child I love so much make such destructive choices, and what did I do that caused the situation?

We as parents do face difficult issues that affect our kids, such as:

- marital problems.
- abuse in the home from which we don't know how to protect the kids.
- choosing to remarry after a divorce and bringing step-children into the home
- dealing with a special needs child and the stress that it can bring to the whole family.
- dealing with a strong-willed child, as a single parent especially.
- illness of one parent or of a child in the family.
- being a people-pleaser and not establishing firm boundaries.

We are not responsible for the choices our kids make. We are only responsible for our actions and reactions, as they are for theirs. While the pain of things in childhood cause feelings of rejection and the hole in the soul that some people try to fill with drugs and alcohol, it ultimately comes down to making healthy choices or unhealthy ones.

What can we do with guilt and remorse?

1. Understand our position in Christ. Jesus died so that we may have life: joyful, rich, abundant life (John 10:10). We are not defined by our past.

    ..old things have passed away; all things have become new (2 Corinthians 5:17).

    We have a bright future, a blessed present, and a new past.
2. Acknowledge choices that we made that have hurt our kids. Be honest and ask forgiveness for things that we could have done better, if anything.
3. Trust God to bring beauty from ashes (Isaiah 61:3). Know how much He loves your kids, just as He loves you: unconditionally, deeply, personally. There is nothing you can do to make Him love you any more or any less. Release the past and the regrets. Live in freedom today. Allow Him to work in their lives in His time and in His way.
4. Don't let guilt feelings cause you to enable your children. It is important for them to see you acting in healthy ways now and holding firmly to boundaries. It will not be popular but it is crucial for their growth as well as yours.
5. Find your identity as the daughter of The King, not as 'Mom'. There is no greater privilege in life than being a mother, but it will destroy us if that becomes our primary identity. We can't control our kids and their choices.

We all make wrong decisions in life. God does not call us to live in bondage to those decisions.

QUESTIONS:

1. How does feeling guilty relate to enabling?

2. Do you feel responsible for your child's addiction? Are you responsible? Discuss.

3. What is the solution for our guilt and remorse over decisions we have made that have affected our children?

4   Is there anything for which you need to apologize? What does a healthy apology look like?

5   How do we gain freedom from guilt and remorse? What does Romans 8:1,2 say?   If there is no condemnation because of what Jesus Christ did for us, do we need to live with the pain of guilt and remorse?

PRAYER:

Father, it is so easy to feel the sting of guilt and remorse when we see our kids struggling with addiction. We know our humanness and our flaws as parents. But you gave Jesus so that we are no longer under condemnation. You have called us to walk in freedom and grace. Teach us, Lord, to accept and believe that we not only have a future with You and Your presence with us now, but You gave us a new past when You made all things new. Thank you for Your amazing love.

Chapter 13

FEAR

"I am afraid my child will overdose and die." "I fear my child will end up in prison for dealing drugs." "It scares me that my child will get beaten up and/or raped in prison." "I am afraid he will get stabbed or shot during a drug deal gone bad." "I am terrified that my child will prostitute herself or himself to get money for drugs." "I am afraid my child will get pregnant/get STDs because of this lifestyle."

These are very real fears and are part of life in addiction. When my son was beaten up by a drug dealer and had his collarbone broken, I was stunned and devastated. When I found out that he was using heroin, I knew that he was just one bag away from death each time he used. I also knew that there was nothing I could do to make him stop destroying himself other than continually praying for him.

Where can I go with these fears? Walk back with me 2,000 years to see a heavy, rough, wooden cross, one of the most cruel and torturous ways to die, and see the perfect Son of God in agony on that cross so that my son and daughter could live. Is He worthy of my trust? Yes! Is He working in their lives, whether I see it or not? Yes! Does He care about this fear that grips me and drives me to torrents of tears? Yes! He died so that we might live. He lives so that we may experience life to the fullest, regardless of our circumstances.

The thief comes only to steal and kill and destroy. I came that they may have life, and have it abundantly (John 10:10).

When we truly release our children to God, to give up our claims to the kind of life we want for them (and for ourselves), we can finally have a safe place to relinquish our fears—into the loving arms of our Papa, the God who is love. Romans 8:32 says,

> *He who did not spare His own Son, but delivered Him over for us all, how will He not also with Him freely give us all things?*

Although those things we fear may ultimately come true, our peace and our hope are in Christ alone. We can trust that He is working in our child's life, no matter what it looks like. Isaiah 41:10 says,

> *Do not fear, for I am with you; do not anxiously look about you, for I am your God. I will strengthen you, surely I will help you, surely I will uphold you with My righteous right hand* (NASB).

Notice that God does not promise to take us out of our circumstances but He does promise to keep us through the circumstances. Our fear puts our circumstances up on a pedestal as if they are 'god'. Fear is not supposed to control us; only God is in control. Fear can destroy us in the same way that the drugs/alcohol are destroying our children. The I AM with you is big! When we are fearful, we feel all alone, but that is a lie straight from the enemy of our souls. God is with us. He will NEVER forsake us.

> *Come to Me, all who are weary and heavy-laden, and I will give you rest. Take My yoke upon you and learn from Me, for I am gentle and humble in heart, and you will find rest for your souls. For My yoke is easy and My burden is light* (Matt 11:28-30).

QUESTIONS:

1. In Matthew 11: 28-30, what does Jesus mean when He says, *My yoke is easy and My burden is light*? Does that mean that this life will always be good for us?

2. Read Psalm 91. What pictures does the psalmist paint of your safety in God?

3. Has your child ever overdosed? What is your biggest fear in knowing your child is using drugs or drinking?

4. Our enemy, Satan, is the father of lies. He would like nothing more than to destroy us, and fear is one of his most potent weapons. What are some ways we can combat his lies, even in our darkest times?

PRAYER:

Father, I choose to trust you in every circumstance, no matter how dark and scary it is. You will not fail me or forsake me. I give you my fear in exchange for Your peace.

Chapter 14

DISAPPOINTMENT

Disappoint: to fail to fulfill the expectations or wishes of. To defeat the fulfillment of hopes, plans, etc. To thwart or frustrate (Webster's Dictionary).

Let's face it; when we give birth to beautiful children, the last thing we think about is having them become addicts. We expect that they will finish school, graduate from college, get a job, find a good wife or husband, and raise a family of our grandchildren. We expect them to work hard, study hard, and play hard.

When our world comes crashing down with the realization that our child has chosen a destructive path of addiction, where do we go with our pain and disappointment? We can not force our children to do what we want them to do or to be what we want them to be. We can't control them. It doesn't work.

Many mothers find their identity in their kids' accomplishments, which is a path of pain even in otherwise 'good' situations. The minute we find our significance and identity in any human being, we are doomed to disappointment. People let us down, including (and maybe especially) those that we birthed.

The only solid foundation for our identity comes from the One who created us, loves us unconditionally, and died to free us from the penalty of our sin. That One is Jesus. We no longer need to be defined by the externals of position, possessions, and people once we understand that the God of the Universe loves us passionately. Our identity comes from being a child of The King, a princess of the Most High, not because of what we do but because of who He is. He covers us with His beautiful clothing of righteousness so that we do not have to feel shame.

Does it hurt and disappoint us when our kids make disastrous choices? Absolutely. But it does not have to destroy us if our foundation is solid in Jesus Christ.

There is a wonderful website called *The Father's Love Letter*. I highly recommend it to anyone, especially if you are struggling with your identity and are not feeling loved. There is a transcript of it in the Appendix but it is worth seeing the video on the website: http://www.fathersloveletter.com

QUESTIONS:

1. What were your expectations when your child was born? For yourself? For your child? For your family?

2. Describe the disappointment you have experienced throughout your child's addiction. How have you coped with this disappointment?

3. Where does your joy come from when you feel sad and disappointed because of choices your child has made?

— Read James 1:2. What does it say about joy?

— Read Romans 15:13. What is our source of hope?

4. On what is your identity based? Job, home, possessions, children, education, church work/ministry? What should your identity be based upon?

PRAYER:

Father, it is so easy to feel disappointment when I put my hope in anything or anyone besides You. My identity needs to be only in You and not in my child.

Chapter 15

BROKENNESS

It has been said that pain is the touchstone of change. Until our kids have experienced enough pain in their addiction, until they have lost everything that mattered to them, until they recognize that their way doesn't work, they will not change.

Brokenness means coming to the end of one's self because of reaching a place of pain, destruction, and despair. It is recognizing that freedom is only found in finally saying, *not my will but Yours be done.* This is exactly what addicts do NOT want to do. They are in such slavery that they actually fear being clean and sober. They will continue on their path until the pain of staying the same becomes greater than the pain of changing.

Our job is to assist them to brokenness. This does not involve screaming at them or subjecting them to long lectures about their behavior, because they are quite capable of tuning us out or giving lip-service to change while doing whatever they want to do. It also does not mean that we stop loving them and expressing love to them. Assisting them to brokenness means:

1. not allowing them to live with us while they are using
2. not giving them money
3. not giving them rides
4. not paying their rent
5. not giving them food
6. not paying their phone bill

7. not bailing them out of jail
8. not paying their fines
9. not paying for lawyers for them
10. not believing them when they say they will change if they can just come home to live.

In essence, it means taking our hands off of them, letting them stay in life's 'time-out chair', and allowing God to work in their life through pain so that they reach the place of surrender. We keep God in handcuffs, so to speak, when we constantly interfere with what He wants to do in their lives.

Perhaps part of the problem is that we haven't reached the place of brokenness ourselves. We still think we have to play God and rescue our kids because we don't trust Him to work in them. When we reach the point of brokenness where we trust Him completely, He can work in our lives to mold us into the godly mother our kids need to see.

Have you ever done any pottery or watched someone work with clay? A shapeless lump can be transformed by a skilled potter into a work of art, and yet often times the emerging pot has to be broken down to the lump state if the process is not going well. It is only then that the potter can remake the clay into something beautiful and useful. We can trust our Father to gently and skillfully take our brokenness and make it into His work of art, if we let Him.

QUESTIONS:

1. Why do you think addicts fear being clean and sober?

2. What can we do to allow our children to stay in the 'time-out chair' so that God can work with them? What things do we do that interfere with our children reaching brokenness?

3. Read Isaiah 64:8. If we all are the work of His Hand, how can that truth change our perspective on trusting Him with our precious children?

PRAYER:

Change my heart, Oh God; make it ever true.
Change my heart, Oh God; may I be like You.
You are the potter, I am the clay;
Mold me and make me. This is what I pray.

Lyrics by Eddie Espinosa

Chapter 16

FORGIVENESS

A person in addiction will do and say things that are extremely hurtful, beyond anything you would have ever imagined. You may reach a point where you hurt so badly that you don't want anything to do with your child. The thought of forgiveness may seem beyond the realm of possibility.

Does forgiveness mean that you accept his behavior? Does it mean that you take her in and allow your child to continue hurting you on a daily basis? Does your child have to ask for forgiveness in order for you to forgive them?

Forgiveness does not mean condoning harmful, hurtful behavior. There is a difference between setting boundaries and holding on to grudges. Your child may never get to the place where she is healthy enough to recognize what she has done. Learning to forgive in the face of unrepentance is for your health, not your child's. When you hold on to bitterness, you poison your soul and imprison it behind bars of unforgivingness that destroy your peace, joy, and love; it can also affect other relationships in your life.

What are the reasons to forgive?

1. God forgave us. 1 John 1:9 says,

    If we confess our sins, He is faithful and just to forgive our sins and cleanse us from all unrighteousness.

    He asks us to forgive those who do wrong to us, just as He forgives us.

2. Forgiveness frees us from the past and allows us to love the unloveable.

3. Forgiveness allows for the possibility of reconciliation if your child repents.

4. Forgiveness keeps our hearts from being destroyed by someone else's behavior, even though we don't condone that behavior.

5. Forgiveness comes from humility. We think we have a right to be treated in a certain way and when that is violated, we think we have a right to bring about justice. The wrong that has been done to us has really been done to God. David, in Psalm 51, says *against You and You alone have I sinned*. When we harbor unforgivingness, we make the person who has harmed us an idol.

   Colossians 3: 12-13 says:

   Put on then, as God's chosen ones, holy and beloved, compassionate hearts, kindness, humility, meekness, and patience, bearing with one another, forgiving each other; as the Lord has forgiven you, so you also must forgive.

There is a difference between forgiveness and reconciliation. One of the definitions of reconciliation is to restore friendship or harmony. Reconciliation can occur when people acknowledge that they have hurt you, apologize for their behavior, and take steps that show they are sincere about change.

Once we have forgiven (which may be a process over time), we can then truly love and accept our children right where they are. That does not mean we accept wrong behavior but we accept the people God made our children to be.

Mary Ann Kiernan, in the book *Crossing the Jordan*, says,

When you refuse to forgive, you give power over your life to another individual. Chains of unforgivingness bind you and affect all areas of your life—emotionally, physically and spiritually.

Do you want to be free? The choice is yours.

QUESTIONS:

1. What are some examples of things that have been difficult for you to forgive relating to your child's addiction? Is there anything your child has done that you feel is unpardonable?

2. Tony Robbins said, *Forgiveness is a gift you give yourself.* Do you agree or disagree? Why or why not?

3. If I forgive my child, does that mean I am enabling him or her to continue in addiction? Why or why not?

4. Does forgiving someone mean that he or she does not have to feel the consequences of his or her choices?

5. On a practical level, what is the difference between forgiveness and reconciliation?

6. Is there anyone else in your life whom you need to forgive? If so, what holds you back from forgiving that person?

PRAYER:

Father, You have forgiven me for so much and yet so often I hold on to unforgivinness toward other people who have wounded me. Please help me to forgive as You forgive, and may I experience freedom to love that person as a result.

Chapter 17

BODY CARE

We were designed by God to have three parts: body, soul, and spirit (I Thes. 5:23). Our spirit is the part of us that relates to God. Our soul, the seat of our personality, is made up of our mind, will, and emotions. Our bodies were designed to be our *earthsuit*, as Bill Gillham calls it in his book *Lifetime Guarantee*. They are the part of us that interacts with the world around us.

When we deal with a child in addiction, our bodies feel the effect of the stress. Long-term stress has a very negative effect on our body.

WebMD.com says,

> *Stress that continues without relief can lead to a condition called distress—a negative stress reaction. Distress can lead to physical symptoms including headaches, upset stomach, elevated blood pressure, chest pain, and problems sleeping. Research also suggests that stress can bring on or worsen certain symptoms or diseases.*

Stress, although not the only cause of any of these problems, has been linked to skin disorders, arthritis, acid reflux, and asthma, as well as emotional disorders such as depression and anxiety.

In order for stress to have the least negative impact on our earthsuits, it is important for us to provide a strong foundation for our physical function. When I was growing up, there was an advertisement for Wonder Bread that claimed to *build strong bodies 12 ways.* There are ways that we can build strong bodies in order to withstand the effects of stress.

Nutrition—There is so much information about what we should eat and how much we eat and when we eat it, to the point where it becomes overwhelming. The pillars of good nutrition are eating low fat, low sugar, limited processed food, moderate portions, multiple small meals per day, sufficient hydration with water, and generous helpings of fruits and veggies. Eliminating or strongly limiting soft drinks from your diet is very important, as the ill effects of soft drink consumption, including diet soda, are well documented.

Exercise—Not only does exercise build body strength and endurance, it provides emotional release, positive mood changes, and better sleep patterns. Something as simple as a 20-minute walk can make a major difference.

Rest/Sleep—Allowing enough time in your schedule for healthy sleep makes a big difference in handling stress. We are more likely to act instead of react when we are rested. Studies show that sleep is extremely important to overall health but is often neglected. It is important to have a day of rest and relaxation each week. God designed our bodies to function best when we have a day that is not filled with work. Moms are often not good about taking the needed time to refresh themselves. Matthew 11:28,30 says,

> *Come to Me, all who are weary and heavy-laden, and I will give you rest. Take My yoke upon you and learn from Me, for I am gentle and humble in Heart, and You will find rest for your souls. For My yoke is easy and My burden is light.*

Because stress affects our body and soul, it is important to develop management techniques that can help us deal with stress in a positive way, such as:

- Praise, prayer, and meditation—Finding strength, solitude, and serenity through meditation on God's Word, praying about every detail of our life, reading and memorizing Scripture, and praising God no matter what happens focuses our minds on God and not on our circumstances. Isaiah 26:3 says,

  You will keep (her) in perfect peace whose mind is stayed on You, because (she) trusts in You.

- Relaxation—This could be reading a good book, going to the beach or pool, listening to music, or watching a good, non-stressful TV show.

- Recreation/Hobby—Find something you enjoy doing or further develop a skill you already have.

- Receiving emotional support from friends, family, and a support group. Finding people with whom you can be transparent and developing, as Jeff Van Vonderan says it, *grace-full* relationships are key components to relieving stress. Grace-full relationships provide an atmosphere of safety and transparency and let you know you are not alone on this journey.

We need a connection with a caring, compassionate body of believers in a church to encourage our love relationship with God. Praise, worship, teaching, and transparent fellowship have the added benefit of relieving the drudgery of stress and lifting us beyond our situation.

QUESTIONS:

1. What are some negative ways that stress related to your child's addiction has affected your body?

2. What are some changes you can make in how you deal with stress?

3. How is transparency in relationships vital in relieving stress?

PRAYER:

Father, I know that I don't always take care of my body the way You would want me to. I ask You to help me make the right decisions to take care of this body You have given me.

Chapter 18

SPIRIT CARE

Have you ever stood outside on a clear, dark winter night and looked at the billions of stars above you? How did you feel (besides cold!)? Small, insignificant, as if you could not possibly matter in the big scheme of things? Or perhaps you have seen a towering mountain and felt like an ant in comparison. How could the God who created the multitudes of stars and the enormity of mountains care about me and my problems? With all the billions of people on the earth and all who have lived before us, why would what I am going through even be noticed by God?

The truth is that the God of the Universe, Creator of the majestic and the complex, designed you to be His child, to be in a loving, intimate relationship with Him. Psalm 139: 15,16 says:

My frame was not hidden from you, when I was being made in secret, intricately woven in the depths of the earth. Your eyes saw my unformed substance; in your book were written, every one of them, the days that were formed for me, when as yet there was none of them.

God created us to have three parts that make each of us uniquely who we are. We have a body, which relates to the world around us. We have a soul, made up of our mind, will, and emotions. And we have a spirit, which is the part of us made to relate to God. Because our genetic makeup came originally from Adam and Eve, and because they chose to destroy the perfect world they lived in by disobeying God in the one thing He asked them not to do, our spirits died in the Garden of Eden. But here is the good news! God wasn't done with humans back then and He isn't done with us now. He sent His Son, Jesus, to live on this earth, to be brutally tortured and killed, and to come back to life from the dead so that we could have new spirits. He paid the price for our sin so that we can have an intimate, loving relationship—a spirit relationship—with the God of the universe. Read Romans 6:23.

What is our part in all of this? We have all been offered a gift—no more penalty for our sin, a loving relationship with our Abba (Papa), and eternal life. But none of that is possible until we receive the gift. Someone could buy us the most amazing Christmas gift, wrap it beautifully, and put our name on the tag, but until we actually claim it as ours, it does us no good. God is waiting for you to take His gift, no matter who you are or what you have done. When you receive Jesus as your Savior and your Lord, your identity is now "Child of God, Princess of The Most High".

It is said that when John F. Kennedy was president of the United States, the most powerful nation in the world, his days were filled with many important people wanting his time. Yet his son, John-John, could run into the Oval Office and climb up on his daddy's lap whenever he wanted to do so. He had a special relationship with the most powerful man in the world that allowed him instant access. That is what God offers to you. Sound good?

You may already have a relationship with God but feel as if He has deserted you in a time of terrible pain. You may have prayed and prayed for your child to stop doing the things that are so destructive but you haven't seen an answer so far. The truth is that God allows pain in our lives to *crowd us to Christ*. He allows everything that we have made an idol in our life to be taken away so that we learn that He is all we need. God created us to be in a love relationship with Him.

He cares about every intimate detail of your life. Our job is to surrender everything so that we can gain everything: peace, joy, unconditional love, contentment, and a relationship with God that nothing can break. We are then free to love our child to life.

QUESTIONS:

1. The most important decision you can make is to receive Jesus as your Lord and Savior. How does that decision relate to the problems you are having with a child in addiction?

2. Read 2 Corinthians 5:14,15,21. What do those verses mean to you?

3. Read Romans 8:32. Does the promise that God will *freely give us all things* necessarily mean that our kids will find freedom from addiction?

PRAYER:

Father, I know that I make a mess of things and sin even when I don't want to. I receive the gift of your Son, Jesus, as my Savior and Lord and give all that I am—past, present, and future—to you. Thank you for saving me and for giving me a new spirit so that I can live with you forever.

Chapter 19

SOUL CARE

When we receive Jesus as Lord and Savior, we are given the gift of a brand new spirit and eternal life in a love relationship with God. We have the Holy Spirit living in us as our guide, friend, comforter, and counselor.

Picture a peach—the pit (seed), which represents life, is at the core of the fruit, just as your spirit is at the core of your being. Around the seed is the flesh of the peach, which is equivalent to our soul. The soul is made up of our mind, will, and emotions and is the part of us that relates to other people. The skin of the peach represents the physical body. All three sections affect each other. The spirit relates to God and is the source of peace and joy in our lives. The soul is the main battleground, because the enemy, Satan, does not want us to show the beauty and sweetness of the life in the spirit. He would rather we be hard, sour, mealy, or full of worm holes. Even though we have new life in us, we still hang on to those old patterns of what we call 'flesh'—anger, self-centeredness, blaming, people-pleasing, worry, fear, guilt, insecurity, doubt, or inferiority feelings. We try to be good moms, good wives, good daughters, good workers, even good church workers. We try to keep our kids from making wrong choices and try to control them when they do. We try and try and try. And all the while God is saying to us, "Stop trying and start trusting."

It is only when we are broken that God can work in us. It is in the surrender of absolutely everything in our life that His peace, His joy, and His love can shine in our soul. God uses tough circumstances to 'crowd us to Christ'. Brokenness sounds like a bad thing but it is the gateway to real life. It is only when I give up my claim to my rights to myself that real life can begin.

Does this mean that everything in life will be 'peachy' and that our kids will suddenly stop being addicts and do the right things? It would be wonderful if that happened but don't count on it. They have to come to their own point of brokenness; we can not force them to get there. What they desperately need is to see a mom who has surrendered everything to God and who is allowing the beauty of a new spirit, the spirit of life in Christ Jesus, to shine in her. They need a mom whose identity is in Christ and not in her kids. They need a mom who is consistent in loving and forgiving without enabling.

QUESTIONS:

1. People-pleasing is a very common issue among people dealing with an addict. Why do you think this is a problem?

2. What other flesh patterns listed in the second paragraph have you experienced? How have they affected you? How have they affected other people in your life?

3. Why is it important for a mom dealing with an addicted child to be healthy in every area of her life?

PRAYER:

Father, I know that the enemy wants me to stay in the old flesh patterns instead of allowing the beauty of Jesus to live through me. So much of the time what I do looks good to others but it is really all about me. I give up my claim to my right to myself so that You can live Your life through me.

APPENDIX

Appendix

My Child...

You may not know me, but I know everything about you. Psalm 139:1   I know when you sit down and when you rise up. Psalm 139:2   I am familiar with all your ways. Psalm 139:3   Even the very hairs on your head are numbered. Matthew 10:29-31 For you were made in my image. Genesis 1:27   In me you live and move and have your being. Acts 17:28   For you are my offspring. Acts 17:28   I knew you even before you were conceived. Jeremiah 1:4-5 I chose you when I planned creation. Ephesians 1:11-12   You were not a mistake, for all your days are written in my book. Psalm 139:15-16   I determined the exact time of your birth and where you would live. Acts 17:26   You are fearfully and wonderfully made. Psalm 139:14 I knit you together in your mother's womb. Psalm 139:13   And brought you forth on the day you were born. Psalm 71:6   I have been misrepresented by those who don't know me. John 8:41-44   I am not distant and angry, but am the complete expression of love. 1 John 4:16 And it is my desire to lavish my love on you. 1 John 3:1   Simply because you are my child and I am your Father. 1 John 3:1   I offer you more than your earthly father ever could. Matthew 7:11   For I am the perfect father. Matthew 5:48   Every good gift that you receive comes from my hand. James 1:17   For I am your provider and I meet all your needs. Matthew 6:31-33 My plan for your future has always been filled with hope. Jeremiah 29:11 Because I love you with an everlasting love. Jeremiah 31:3   My thoughts toward you are countless as the sand on the seashore. Psalms 139:17-18   And I rejoice over you with singing. Zephaniah 3:17   I will never stop doing good to you. Jeremiah 32:40 For you are my treasured possession. Exodus 19:5   I desire to establish you with all my heart and all my soul. Jeremiah 32:41   And I want to show you great and marvelous things. Jeremiah 33:3 If you seek me with all your heart, you will find me. Deuteronomy 4:29   Delight in me and I will give you the desires of your heart. Psalm 37:4   For it is I who gave you those desires. Philippians 2:13   I am able to do more for you than you could possibly imagine. Ephesians 3:20   For I am your greatest encourager. 2 Thessalonians 2:16-17 I am also the Father who comforts you in all your troubles. 2 Corinthians 1:3-4   When you are brokenhearted, I am close to you. Psalm 34:18   As a shepherd carries a lamb, I have carried you close to my heart. Isaiah 40:11 One day I will wipe away every tear from your eyes. Revelation 21:3-4   And I'll take away all the pain you have suffered on this earth. Revelation 21:3-4   I am your Father, and I love you even as I love my son, Jesus. John 17:23 For in Jesus, my love for you is revealed. John 17:26   He is the exact representation of my being. Hebrews 1:3   He came to demonstrate that I am for you, not against you. Romans 8:31   And to tell you that I am not counting your sins. 2 Corinthians 5:18-19   Jesus died so that you and I could be reconciled. 2 Corinthians 5:18-19   His death was the ultimate expression of my love for you. 1 John 4:10   I gave up everything I loved that I might gain your love. Romans 8:31-32   If you receive the gift of my son Jesus, you receive me. 1 John 2:23   And nothing will ever separate you from my love again. Romans 8:38-39   Come home and I'll throw the biggest party heaven has ever seen. Luke 15:7   I have always been Father, and will always be Father. Ephesians 3:14-15   My question is...Will you be my child? John 1:12-13 I am waiting for you. Luke 15:11-32

Love, Your Dad

Almighty God

* Words paraphrased from the Holy Bible ©1999-2008 FathersLoveLetter.com

CODEPENDENCY CHECKLIST

This checklist was compiled by Melody Beattie, author of *Codependent No More*.

- Do you feel responsible for other people—their feelings, thoughts, actions, choices, wants, needs, well-being and destiny?

- Do you feel compelled to help people solve their problems or by trying to take care of their feelings?

- Do you find it easier to feel and express anger about injustices done to others than about injustices done to you?

- Do you feel safest and most comfortable when you are giving to others?

- Do you feel insecure and guilty when someone gives to you?

- Do you feel empty, bored and worthless if you don't have someone else to take care of, a problem to solve, or a crisis to deal with?

- Are you often unable to stop talking, thinking, and worrying about other people and their problems?

- Do you lose interest in your own life when you are in love?

- Do you stay in relationships that don't work and tolerate abuse in order to keep people loving you?

- Do you leave bad relationships only to form new ones that don't work, either?

TESTIMONIES

M's STORY

Sometime around 1992 my world began to come apart at the seams. My marriage was in the pits and my teenage sons were getting out of control. They were using drugs and alcohol, failing in school, and had become strangers to me. All I could think was, "How did I get to this place? Why was this happening to me?" I was selfish, depressed, angry, and hopeless. The pity pot was where I made my home.

In 1992, I could not have imagined, even in my wildest dreams, that the addiction that seemed to be destroying my sons' lives would be the very thing that would save me, my marriage, and my family. In time, I came to understand God would use addiction to open my eyes to Truth—His Truth.... but this would take another six long years. God will get our attention one way or another. I had been ignoring His prompting in my life for years. Jesus said

No one can come to me unless the Father who sent me draws him... John 6:44.

He was getting my attention now! I was so fearful that I could barely function and cried most of each day away. In my hopeless thoughts, I saw only three possibilities:

1. My sons would die of an overdose.
2. They would kill themselves or someone else in a car accident.
3. They would end up in jail.

You see, I had lost all hope that they would ever be free from addiction.

I didn't grow up in a Christian home. My Momma was Russian Orthodox and my Poppa was Lutheran. My older siblings and I were brought up in the Lutheran Church. We talked about God once in a while at home but 'religion' and God were more of a tradition than anything else. For me, church, God, and Jesus were separate from the 'real' world. It all seemed more like a myth than fact. In church, I never heard about a 'relationship with Jesus', that I needed to be born again, or exactly what that meant. By the time I was married and had my sons, my church attendance had become less and less frequent. Around the time I was 35, I was dragging my family to church for Christmas and Easter just to 'do the right thing'.

In 1991, my 81-year-old Pop was in the hospital and dying. After three days of being at his bedside and crying constantly, I was spent, exhausted and didn't have anything more to give. My Momma and three sisters were in worse shape than me. I stepped out of his hospital room, slipped down on the floor, and cried out to God to help me be there for my Pop, to give me the strength that I didn't have to get through this difficult time, and help me to do what needed to be done in the days ahead. Even though I wasn't a believer at the time, I believe that God answered my prayer. As clear and instantaneous as a bell, I felt all my fear, anxiety, and overwhelming grief lift from me. I stood up, went in to be with my Pop, and took charge of all that was going on at that time and even after his death. I believe that God answered my prayer because He was trying to get my attention to draw me to Himself. Unfortunately, I would need to go through many more trials until I finally surrendered my life to Him.

After my Poppa's death, everything changed in my life. My parents were older immigrants from Ukraine. My Momma had very little education, spoke very little English, didn't drive and couldn't live alone. John and I sold our home, built onto her home, and moved our family in. I lost my home, my freedom, my privacy, and, basically, became Momma's 'little girl' again. Our mother/daughter relationship deteriorated and became volatile. Within two years of moving in, John and Daniel were well on their way into the drug world and my marriage was hitting some all time lows.

By the time the fall of 1994 rolled around, I didn't think things could be much worse, even though my younger son Daniel (16 at the time) was going into a 28 day secular rehab. A big sign welcomed us as we dropped him off; it read, "Expect a Miracle". But no miracle was to be found there. Oh...God was definitely getting my attention! I knew I needed God in my life and that was just about all I knew at the time.

A new friend of mine invited me to her church. This church was warm and friendly. A small group of born-again believers took me 'under their wings'. They didn't know anything about addiction and couldn't give me any help or direction in regard to it. What they did do was invite me to adult Sunday school, a Bible study, love me, and pray for my family and me....oh how they prayed! I slowly began to see that the deep gaping hole in my heart could only be filled by God. I was beginning to understand what a relationship with Christ meant. Those 'born again believers' were not some crazy Bible thumpers with daisies in their hands! I was learning and growing.

It wasn't until March, 1998, when Daniel entered the Colony of Mercy and I began to attend chapel services (Sunday evening, Wednesday evening TNT and, back at that time, Friday evening service) that I really 'heard' what I needed to do to get right with God and ask Christ into my heart. I kept thinking I had to get my life right, clean my own act up so to speak before I could ask a righteous and Holy Savior into my heart. But Jerry Rusco's booming voice kept ringing in my ears that there was nothing I could do to earn my salvation. There was nothing I could do change my life in my own will power. I needed to recognize my sinful, lost

condition, confess, repent, and accept Christ as my Savior....
He would take care of the rest.

In my Bible studies I was learning so much about myself,
marriage, and about trusting God in the midst of trials. I
was even learning something very profound...I was NOT in
control...not of my marriage, not of my sons' sobriety, and
certainly not even of myself! Everything I read in God's Word
was telling me my problems began with me. I needed to
change my heart and my behavior and stop trying to change
John, my sons, and everyone else. The book of Ephesians was
having a great impact on my heart.

> *You were taught, with regard to your former way of life,
> to put off your old self, which is being corrupted by its
> deceitful desires; to be made new in the attitude of your
> minds; and to put on the new self, created to be like God in
> true righteousness and holiness* (Eph. 4:22-24)

Instead of trying to change every one else, I was the one that
needed to change.

God was asking me to surrender everything to Him...my
broken marriage, my broken family, my broken relationship
with my Momma, and my sons' addiction.

Daniel graduated from the Colony of Mercy July 4th,
1998. I had high hopes. Within a month, he was using again,
out of control, and I was crushed. We had tickets to the Sight
and Sound Theater to see *Noah* in October of 1998. While
Daniel was in the Colony, he insisted that we get tickets
for the whole family. Once again I had high hopes. Surely
this would 'bring him to his senses and have an impact on
our other son'. The day was filled with anxiety and tears
until I sat down in the theater. When I left that theater...I
left as a new creation in Christ! At the end of *Noah*, Christ
descended from the 'heavens' with His arms wide open. I
was so overwhelmed with emotion, I finally understood I
could do nothing to clean up my heart; that was His job. I

couldn't 'fix' my marriage and love my husband, but Christ could do it though me. My relationship with my Momma could be 'fixed' by Christ alone. I couldn't 'fix' my sons; only Christ could save them, and they were in His loving hands. I finally 'got it'—confessed, repented, and accepted Jesus as my Savior. I would love to tell you God repaired all of it...instantly. But that isn't the way it happened. First I was made a new creation in Christ. Second, my marriage was reborn in November, 1998. Daniel re-entered the Colony in August, 2000, and has been walking with the Lord in victory ever since. Just prior to my Momma's death in 2002, we were able to make our peace with one another. Many unanswered prayers are still lifted up in faith.

God had tried many ways to get my attention....addiction got my attention and now all these years later, I'm grateful for it, because God has used it in a powerful way in the life on my family. God used all my junk and turned it into treasure for my good and His glory!

> *And we know that in all things God works for the good of those who love him, who have been called according to his purpose* (Romans 8:28).

It might sound crazy to many, but I am grateful because without it I may never have come to know Jesus as my Savior and missed all His blessings for my family.

> *Praise be to the God and Father of our Lord Jesus Christ, the Father of compassion and the God of all comfort, who comforts us in all our troubles, so that we can comfort those in any trouble with the comfort we ourselves have received from God* (2 Cor. 1:3,4)

This verse began to speak to my heart. I heard God saying to me, "Hey, I didn't save you to just sit up on a shelf and look pretty. I saved you so that you could touch the lives of others and comfort them the way I comforted you." I felt called to go back to college (Philadelphia Biblical University). I earned a bachelors degree in Bible and went on to earn a Master's in Christian Counseling. God in His mercy and grace brought me back to America's Keswick in 2005. I had always felt that part of my heart was still here. I started out as a volunteer with the Women's Ministry and now serve as full-time staff as the intake coordinator for the Colony of Mercy. I have a heavy heart for the men lost in addiction and their families. Since my son went through the Colony, I have a special place in my heart for the Colony and the men that find their way to its door. It is a privilege and honor to be used by God in a small way in their road to recovery and freedom from addiction. I still have to pinch myself when I pull into the long Keswick drive...God really does give you the desires of your heart as you seek Him in obedience. And He isn't done with me yet!

> *To Him who is able to do immeasurably more than all we ask or imagine according to His power that is at work within us, to Him be the glory in the church and in Christ Jesus throughout all generations* (Eph. 3:20,21).

Thus far....the Lord has brought me........

K's STORY

My son was 42 years old when he was called to be with Jesus. He was an addict for 20 years. In the beginning I thought I could stop the addiction—I was an ENABLER—big time! I made excuses, gave money, and allowed the disrespect. It didn't happen overnight but with God's help I started to 'let go and let God'. I had to realize I didn't cause it, can't control it, and can't cure his addiction! It was out of my hands and into the hands of God.

I retired and moved to New Jersey from New York, leaving family and friends, and slowly peace came into my life. Through God, I found America's Keswick and the Colony of Mercy Addiction Recovery Center. After praying for three years, my son finally applied for admission to the Colony of Mercy.

I have learned PATIENCE—God has a plan and will work His miracles in His time.

Now that my son has passed, I look at the years of agony for him and for our family. There were four rehabs (to no avail), loss of employment, self-worth, and family. God's plan was for me to move and find Keswick so that Chris would be saved.

The last year of Chris' life was the most wonderful. He was a changed person and very much into the Bible and the Word of God. He was relating to the other men in the Colony. He gave his life to Jesus and through Him was working to spread the word about his new life in Christ. His sense of humor, laughter, and personality were returning. Every day, I thank Jesus for returning my son to me so I could see the man he was supposed to be.

God had a plan for calling Chris home when He did. Chris is now at peace and I look forward to the day when we will meet again.

A's STORY

My Story: Choosing Hope, Not Fear (from a former addict)

Outside looking in, I was the cute little girl that belonged to a big happy family; everything was perfect, and everyone was happy. However, looking inward, I was a hurricane, tearing myself apart, pushing away the people who loved me.

I grew up in a household where I was the youngest of five kids. Anything more than one child means competition:

competition in talents, sports, academics, and attention. I never felt good enough. I thought maybe I'd just do what my family does not. Striving to be different, not just so-and-so's little sister, I did everything that was different than what my family did. I did gymnastics, while my sisters did ballet. I played guitar while my siblings learned piano.

My family loved God, and so I pushed Him away. The more I shut God out, the more blind I became. I was living life like a drunk driver, thinking I'm all good, but I was as good as blind. As I longed for and sought for something to satisfy my heart, I opened my heart to anything that seemed promising. Depression crept its way in, bringing around an eating disorder and self harm to punish myself for not being worth anything. I entered several abusive relationships, but I thought that I deserved what I got, because I was worthless. I cried myself to sleep most nights for many years, wishing that tomorrow I wouldn't wake up.

One night, I fell off my bed and hurt my arm. This is where I found what I believed was the cure for the depression and the hurt and the nightmares. I believed that in this one accident I found the thing that would heal me and make me feel whole. I got a prescription for Percocet. After just two pills, I saved them, because I noticed that when I took a pill, I was happy. I didn't understand why, but I decided that the pain in my heart was far worse than the pain in my arm. After a little while with those, I soon graduated to oxycontin. I had periods of using codeine, Vicodin, and cocaine as well. Unbelievably, after about two years using the pills, I smoked marijuana for my first time, and I told my friend I had never been high before. That's the thing about being a drug addict: I had heard all my life that drug users were bad people. I was not a bad person; I was hurting, this medicine made me happy, and I met other nice people who were sad and took the same medicine as me. In my mind I was a good person, not a drug addict.

I realized pain killers wouldn't cure the depression. Neither would cocaine, or alcohol, or relationships. Every time I opened up to someone, I got hurt, so love was obviously not the cure. I kept throwing up my meals, hurting myself, taking my pills, and drinking myself to sleep. Nothing made me happy and I was sick of it. So I drove home from school one day, with my mind all made up. I went off by myself, and decided to kill myself. If love and drugs couldn't help me, nothing could. If I really was worthless, why even live another second? So quietly and tearfully, I slipped away from the world. I took all the pills I had left, and I smoked a blunt, and then went to stab myself. Then there were footsteps. Then a dog barked. A woman and her dog began to come my way. Embarrassed and terrified that she knew what I was doing, I bolted. I climbed into my car and cried. I screamed out to God, until my throat too sore to handle another a cigarette, begging He would show me why I was alive still.

Addiction causes more than just a dependency on a substance. It causes you to live for nothing and no one but your pill. It becomes your focus, your life goal, your prize. You loose your sense of direction, because it leads you to places you never thought you could end up in. The addiction brings you to a fork in the road, where you must choose to fear it, or choose the hope of overcoming it. They need you to say, "You are not okay, and what you're doing is not okay, but what can I do to help you?" Don't just walk away. They need to know that they are not the worthless pieces of trash the world calls them.

It took three years, but someone finally did that for me. My friend made me realize that Jesus Christ was waiting with arms open wide while I was pushing Him farther away from me. His arms stayed open, outstretched for the embrace of His child. And while His arms were spread, He died for me. While I told Him "I don't need You God, I just need You to leave," He took all my sin, all my tears, all my depression, all my worthlessness, all my drugs, and alcohol, and abuse, and

He nailed it on the cross with Him. He died so suicide didn't have to be the answer for me. He has scars on his wrists so mine didn't have to.

I'm not worthless, and I have a purpose. What I would like you to take away from my story is this: drugs, alcohol, self harm, and eating disorders are all addictions. Addicts need love, not a judgement finger waved in their face. At some point, they opened their heart to something they thought would bring them happiness. When an addict gets to that fork in the road, a little support from one person can cause them to choose hope over fear.

Jesus sees you. He sees when you cry all alone, in the bathroom, in your car, and as you get into bed. He sees the pain your mess is causing you. Jesus saw all of that in me, and He ransomed me. He did more than just that: He chose to LOVE me as well. Read Luke 15. This crazy kid runs off, takes his inheritance, and parties. Then, broken and humiliated, he returns home. While he was still a long way down the road, his father was looking for him, and he saw his son, and ran and embraced him. Sometimes our Father allows our lives to get as crazy as a hurricane, just so we can know what it feels like to come home, and feel his loving embrace. It doesn't matter what you've done, or what they did to you. It doesn't matter how far you ran away from Him. He loves you and desires to have you. When you grasp that concept, you will know exactly why I know now that I am not worthless.

TEA WITH MY BOYS!!!! - LOUISE'S STORY

I first want to tell you that I have prayed to GOD all my life. I really did not know HIM as I do now. I used to dwell on that for quite a long time but I am free now. GOD fixed that for me when I went searching for help for my son who was on drugs; things were getting worse each day. I was told about a young man who was a Pastor in a nearby town who walked the streets talking to young boys and girls who had a problem such as my son did. I met him and made an appointment with him. He and his lovely wife made me feel extremely comfortable while I was telling them about our dilemma. At the end of our conversation he asked if he could pray for Frank and our family. I, of course, said "yes" but I had never prayed out loud before. He started by saying, "Lord, we lift up Doris" and I panicked. He stopped and asked why....my name is Louise.... I thought GOD would not know it was our family. He continued and did take the time to come to talk to our son. Eventually, we joined his church, I was baptized, although my husband was the only one to come to see this because my family thought I was off the beaten track.

Our son was a biker and rode with 21 young men. There were lots of mean and cruel looks from neighbors when they came to our house. I had become close to each and everyone of these boys. They each had a story, and if people would have taken the time to get to know people that did look different and hard they would have learned to love them as I did.

We invited eight of these boys to church one Sunday. I told them if they came to church they could join us for Sunday dinner. Five of them came and sat in the last row of the church and listened to a biker that once belonged to the Warlocks. When the young man was finished speaking, the boys jumped over their seats and ran out of church. They knew what was coming. They did come for dinner and had a feast. Before we started eating, I passed a loaf of bread around and everyone broke off a piece....that stayed with all of us. Each time they came I did have bread. They thought it was cool. Four of them, including my son, came back to church a few more times.

After we got to know each and every one of them, they would call and ask if they could stop and have tea with me. Big six foot boys asking me to come for tea.....who knew. We would sit and talk about the Bible; I felt quite uncomfortable about this for a while because I did not know anything. I would take my Bible and read a few passages and they would listen intently. They would come back quite a bit and spend more time. Then I had to get ready for them to accept the Lord so I wrote the salvation prayer on a little piece of paper and when the first young man said "YES" I immediately took this little paper out my pocket and read it to him. It worked so I continued to do this. I knew GOD was right beside me at that time.

Frank and his friend Mark came one day and told me that they had to talk to me. They had both gone to a clinic to have their blood work done to see if they had any trace of AIDS. They both asked for tea so I thought all was okay. Once they had their tea they told me that they both had the virus. First thing I said to myself was, "GOD please give me the strength and the appropriate words to say to these boys." I shook....and just told them that we would be there for them and pray there was a cure. Weeks after this, more boys came for tea. They had the same news. Out came the little piece of paper with the salvation prayer on it and I explained that one day we will all be in heaven.....no more pain....no more tears, etc. Seventeen bikers accepted the Lord. They still came for tea. They all received hugs. The last boy that came was six feet tall...stocky....polite...kind...he was standing against a wall and slid down onto the floor....so I joined him. Out came the little piece of paper which I still have....we cried...and then had tea.

Soon I was going to wake after wake with my son. I couldn't take too much more when Frank had to be put on Hospice. We took great care of him. Friends did visit him quite a bit, which made him happy. When it was near the end GOD brought the whole family to his bedside....He even brought two special friends and one a nurse. Frank passed away February 20th, 1994. Out of the twenty-one friends, seventeen are gone but I will see them in heaven one day. Thank you, Lord, for always being with me.

HOW TO START A
LOVE THEM TO LIFE (LTTL)
SUPPORT GROUP

Beside Still Waters was written to be used by individual mothers as well as to be the curriculum for a support group for mothers who have children in addiction. Just as mothers have a special bond with their children, so also mothers have a special bond with other mothers who are struggling with the same issues that they are. It is very helpful to be able to join with other mothers and share the pain and problems each are experiencing. Not only do they learn from the topics, they learn from each other. One mother may just be starting on her journey with her child while others have been walking it for years and have a wealth of experience to share.

What does it take to start an LTTL group? It can be as simple as a small group of moms meeting at someone's home. It could be a group sponsored by a church or community center. It is helpful to have one or two people in the group designated as facilitators, in order to have some structure to the group. One does not have to be trained as a counselor or other professional in order to facilitate. It would be helpful to have copies of the book on hand if possible so that each mom could have one.

There is a facilitator's guide available on the *Love Them To Life* website as a free download. It gives suggestions on how to run the group, as well as giving suggested answers to the chapter questions.

We would love to know where the groups are meeting, in case we get women in those areas needing to find a group. Please email us your location, as well as any feedback as to how the group is going or suggestions for improvement to the website and ministry.

RECOMMENDED READING

Families Where Grace is in Place	Jeff VanVonderen
Grace and Addiction	Gerald May, MD
Gracewalk Experience	Steve McVey
Handbook to Happiness *Rejection Syndrome & the Way to Acceptance*	Dr. Charles Solomon
Helping Others Overcome Addictions	Steve McVey and Mike Quarles
Hope and Help for the Addicted	Jeff VanVonderen
Lifetime Guarantee	Dr. Bill Gillham
The Emotionally Destructive Relationship	Leslie Vernick
The Meaning of Marriage	Timothy and Kathy Keller

RESOURCES

Love Them To Life—
lovethemtolife.com. Love Them to Life is a support ministry to mothers of addicts. A list of rehabs is available at our website: This is not an exhaustive list but focuses primarily on Christian rehabs.

Association of Gospel Rescue Missions—
agrm.org/ ARGM has a list of rescue missions in the United States, including contact information.

XL Project—
xlproject.org. XL Project is an outreach ministry to those in addiction and the people who love them.

Grace Fellowship International (GFI)—
gracefellowshipinternational.com. GFI is a ministry of spiritual discipleship, Exchanged Life counseling, and training people-helpers through the message of Christ and the Cross.

Grace Walk Recovery Ministry—
freedomfrom.wordpress.com. The ministry of Mike and Julia Quarles. Mike had many years of addiction to alcohol and was transformed through the message of the Exchanged Life.

America's Keswick Colony of Mercy and Barbara's Place—
americaskeswick.org. Addiction recovery facility in New
Jersey. The Colony of Mercy is a 120-day program for men.
Barbara's Place is a long-term facility for women.

Drug Texting Slang—
noslang.com. A resource website for parents to help them
understand what their children are saying in their texts.

Mayo Clinic—
mayoclinic.com. Search 'drug addiction symptoms'. This is
an excellent article listing all the categories of drugs and their
effects.

How to Be a Child of God—
howtobeachildofGod.com

Hope for the Heart—
hopefortheheart.org. This site has help topics such as alcohol
and drug addiction.

ABOUT THE AUTHOR

He drew me up from the pit of destruction, out of the miry bog, and set my feet upon a rock, making my steps secure. He put a new song in my mouth, a song of praise to our God. Many will see and fear, and put their trust in the Lord (Psalm 40:2,3)

Cherri Freeman and her husband, Joe, have been associates of Grace Fellowship International since April, 2013. Their ministry name, XL Project (for Exchanged Life), is based on the truths of Galatians 2:20 and is used to represent the portion of the GFI ministry which deals with the area of addiction.

Cherri grew up at America's Keswick Colony of Mercy and Conference Center in Whiting, NJ, which was founded by her great grandfather. She graduated from Wheaton College with a BS in biology. Along with working in various medical fields, she taught high school and middle school science for many years. She has raised five children, two of whom struggled with addiction. Her passion is to help other mothers who are dealing with children in addiction, thus birthing the moms' support ministry Love Them To Life (lovethemtolife. com).

Joe attended Trenton State College and graduated from the University of Pittsburgh with a degree in Social Studies. He worked in corporate sales for many years, until his addiction to drugs and alcohol took him, helpless and hopeless, to a one room in a crack hotel with a $1200/day habit and a determination to commit suicide. Through a friend's help, he went to America's Keswick Colony of Mercy, where he surrendered his life to Jesus Christ. His passion is to see others set free from bondage to addiction through the work of

Jesus Christ on the Cross. He is completing a Master's degree in Biblical Counseling from Luther Rice University.

Cherri can be reached by emailing lovethemtolife@gmail.com.

ENDNOTES

Chapter 1:
May, Gerald, MD, *Addiction and Grace* (New York, NY: HarperCollings, 1988), 14, 24.

Chapter 2:
Jeff Van Vonderen, *Hope and Help for the Addicted* (Grand Rapids, MI: Revell, 2004), 55-65.

Chapter 3:
https://www.psychologytoday.com/blog/traversing-the-inner-terrain/201103/king-or-queen-baby

http://korrekt.com/books/king_baby/king_baby.htm

http://www.ask.com/health/king-baby-syndrome-97f93b4141378a4d#full-answer

Chapter 4:
Jeff Van Vonderen, *Hope and Help for the Addicted* (Grand Rapids, MI: Revell, 2004), 83-96.

Chapter 5:
http://www.psychologytoday.com/blog/the-anatomy-addiction/201207/are-you-empowering-or-enabling.

Chapter 14:
http://www.fathersloveletter.com/.

Chapter 16:
Diane Hunt, *Crossing the Jordan* (Fort Washington, PA: CLC Publications, 2011).

Chapter 17:
http://www.webmd.com/mental-health/effects-of-stress-on-your-body.

Bill Gillham, *Lifetime Guarantee* (Eugene, OR: Harvest House Publishers, 1993).

Jeff VanVonderen, *Families Where Grace Is In Place* (Minneapolis, MN: Bethany House, 1992).

Appendix:

http://www.fathersloveletter.com/.

Melody Beattie, *Codependent No More* (Minnesota: Hazeldon Foundation, 19.